HEINZ <u>ULLRICH</u>
& DIETER KLANTE

Creative Metal Design

Reinhold Book Corporation
A subsidiary of Chapman-Reinhold, Inc.

New York   Amsterdam   London

© Otto Maier Verlag, Ravensburg, Germany 1967

Published in the United States of America 1968
by Reinhold Publishing Corporation
Library of Congress Catalog Number 68-20402
Printed in Holland

CONTENTS

INTRODUCTION

Although written for teachers, among others, this is not a school book in the strict sense of the word, for it is also aimed at laymen, youth groups and adult education classes.

Much time and toil have gone into this collection of examples for the encouragement of anyone who wishes to engage in elementary metal work. Processes such as forging, casting and enamelling have been omitted intentionally, as they are difficult to carry out in schools. These may be dealt with in a later publication. As in previous volumes, play is shown to be a means of exercising creative talents.

Since there is ample reason to suspect that many are content slavishly to copy the examples illustrated, it may be useful once again to emphasize the essential nature of play. Play is successful where the means are limited and the course predetermined. The final outcome is unknown and depends on the degree of concentration and the inventiveness exercised by the player. In any event, play is an end in itself. It has no purpose but the pleasure of dealing with certain materials. The player comes to know their properties and gathers experience which in due course will enable him to create useful things, depending on the nature of the substance he is handling. Above all, in time he will learn to discriminate between the good and the bad in the design and quality of goods produced by industry and the crafts.

Ernst Röttger

WORKING WITH METAL

In our technological age, man-made substances increasingly take the place of traditional materials. Yet the various metals still hold their dominant position and are indispensable at the present stage of high technological and industrial development. For thousands of years metal has retained its importance as one of the oldest materials known to man and it has had a decisive influence on our civilisation. It is all the more surprising, therefore, that a material capable of assuming so many shapes is not more often used in creative handicraft. One possible reason may be that people believe it can be worked only by means of special tools and machines. Certainly, the metal industry makes use of the most complicated machinery and highly developed production methods. But even the most modest equipment is capable of producing an inexhaustible variety of artistically interesting objects.

In this book we have selected from the enormous number of metals only those suitable for elementary work. The basic materials are wire, tin and metal fabric. Let us examine their technical qualities and formative possibilities:

Wire as a medium for artistic work has the character of a three-dimensional line which may be arranged on a surface or freely suspended in space. Thus it is the ideal material for three-dimensional objects of a linear character. Wires are available in varying degrees of resistance: soft, medium and hard. We use wires of steel (iron), copper, brass and aluminium, as well as galvanized, copper plated and brass plated wires varying in thickness from 0.2 to 4 mm.

In playing with wire, we learn to appreciate its qualities and experience its hardness, brittleness, forgeability, flexibility and elasticity. Only then do we proceed to particular shapes. The same applies to tin and fabric. Tin has a plane surface. It may be bent, cut and buckled, as, for instance, in the chasing of a vessel. Tin is produced by rollers in thicknesses from 0.2 mm upwards. Tin rolled thinner still is called foil. We mainly use thin metal sheets of aluminium, copper, brass and steel (iron). The best known are sheet iron and tin plate. Very thin tin and especially foil offer little resistance. They can be worked with the simplest of tools, so that even a child may gather elementary experience in metal work.

Wire fabrics are structurally related to textiles. For the purposes of creative play they have the characteristics of a plane, with the special qualities of transparence and lightness. Among other materials, they are made of brass, copper and galvanized wires. For the kind of work described in this book they should not be too wide-meshed. Depending on the structure of the fabric, the possibilities range from alterations to the fabric itself (shifting the wires to vary the width of the mesh, puncturing, fraying, pulling out of wires, bending, cutting, folding) to numerous combinations with wire and tin. Like tin, wire fabric may form a background to some other construction.

Nails, rivets and screws as constructive auxiliary means, have a dotlike character. In conjunction with wire, tin and fabric, they provide the essential features of a picture, i.e. dot, line and surface, while the different metals provide colour.

All these materials are easy and cheap to obtain. It should be remembered that various tins, boxes and packing wires are freely available as waste and extremely useful as basic materials and preformed elements for various purposes, especially those of a constructive nature.

Production methods have been deliberately confined to the simplest techniques. The most 'complicated' tools in our workshop are a soldering-iron and, in a very few instances, a blow-pipe.

Some essential technical tips about materials, tools and methods are summarised at the end of the book.

SYMBOLS USED:

No mark = Work by students of the Pädagogisches Fachinstitut, Kassel

S   = Work by students of the Hochschule für Bildende Künste, Kassel

T   = Work by students in teachers' training colleges

B   = Work by boys

G   = Work by girls

The subsequent numerals indicate the child's age

WORKING WITH WIRE

BENDING

Wire is the most suitable material for gathering elementary experience of metal work. As a three-dimensional line, it expresses direction and movement. The creative process involves not only the eye but also the sense of touch. Fingers bending a wire experience material qualities. Wire may be light or heavy, thick or thin, tough or brittle, and even simple bending reveals innumerable expressive possibilities.

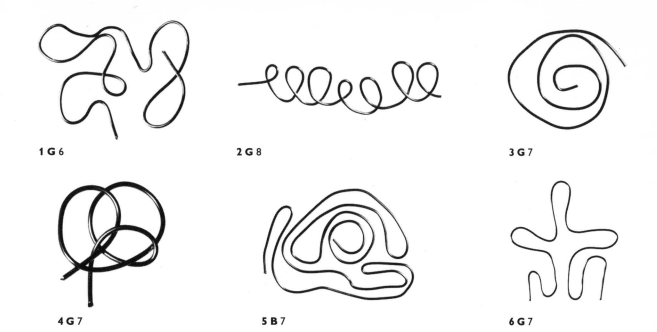

1 G 6   2 G 8   3 G 7

4 G 7   5 B 7   6 G 7

1-6 show simple wire work by children using only their fingers to bend the wires. The most suitable material for this kind of work is soft aluminium wire, 1 mm thick, which offers little resistance to a child's hands. Experimental play with this material produces shapes which correspond to the scribbling stage in drawing. The different steps, as illustrated, are: aimless bending (1); 'garland' (2); spiral (3); loops (4); plane (5;) symbol (6). These spontaneous shapes already contain the germs of elementary methods, discipline and content.

9

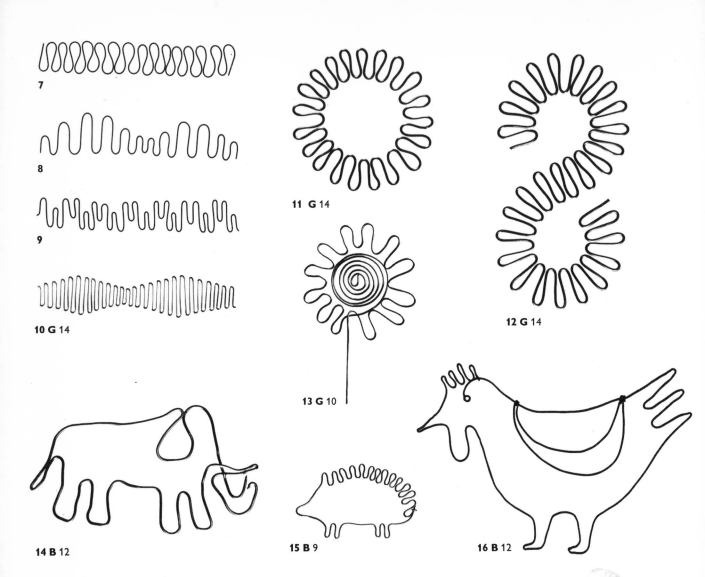

7

8

9

10 G 14

11 G 14

12 G 14

13 G 10

14 B 12

15 B 9

16 B 12

7-10, 17-34: In these exercises the act of bending was controlled by certain rules laid down in advance, e.g. the material, the lines to be followed (round or angular), and the form (ribbon formation). In shaping the wire, the children had to pay attention to an imaginary horizontal centre line or corresponding parallels as lines of reference or limitation.

7: Simple wave structure repeating identical shapes. It is advisable to carry out these exercises by hand only.

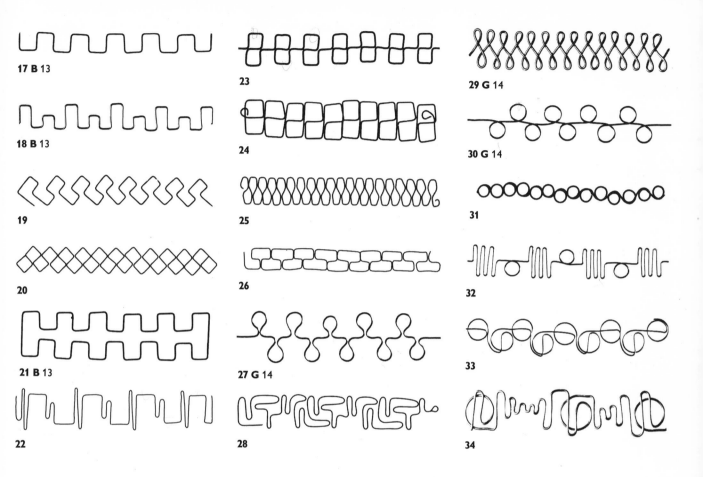

17 B 13 **23** **29 G 14**

18 B 13 **24** **30 G 14**

19 **25** **31**

20 **26** **32**

21 B 13 **27 G 14** **33**

22 **28** **34**

8-10: Variations of the wavy line. Large and small shapes alternate. Increasing and decreasing waves.

11, 12: Wavy wire bent to form open and closed shapes.

14, 16: Wire figures by children. Material: soft aluminium wire.

The character of the lines is partly determined by the tools used. Flat pliers produce angular lines (17-21, 23-26); round pliers and round wooden sticks, softly curving lines (27-34). Materials: galvanized steel wire, 1.2 mm thick; soft aluminium wire, 1 mm thick; binding wire, 0.6 mm thick.

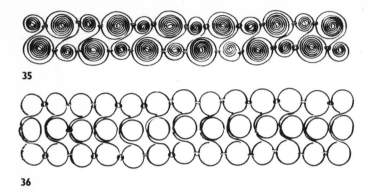

35

37

36

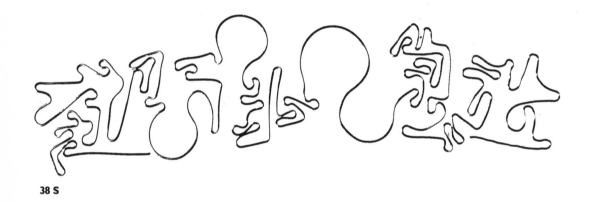

38 S

35: The spiral is a typical wire shape. In this example it provides the basic shape. The spirals were joined by wire rings to form an ornamental band.

36, 37: Regular series of similar shapes. The rings were formed with the help of round wooden sticks; the meander with flat pliers.

38: A figure with strong rhythmical expression.

39, 40: Preliminary exercises for wire ornaments.

41, 42: Regular repetition and loose formation with wire spirals, partly hammered. Material: soft aluminium wire. Tool: round pliers.

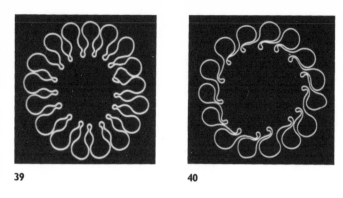

39

40

41

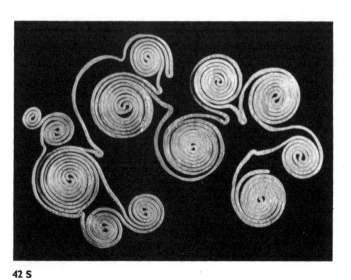

42 S

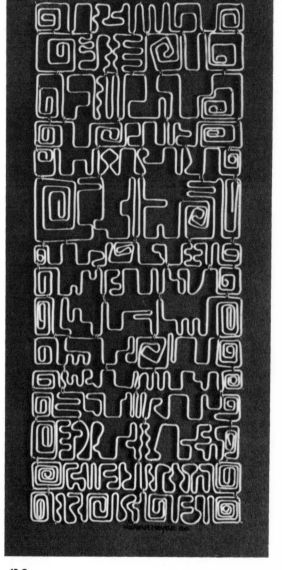

43 S

43: Surface richly ornamented with horizontal bands, joined by rings. Material: aluminium wire, 1 mm thick.

44

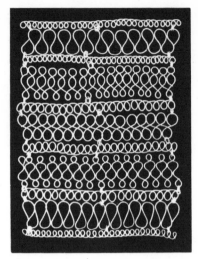

45

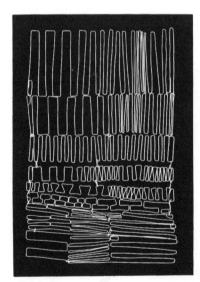

46 S

Pendants of loosely joined wire bands.

44, 45: Variations of wavy lines alternating with narrow and wide wavy bands, partly overlapping. Materials: aluminium wire and galvanized steel wire.

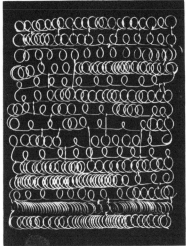

47 S

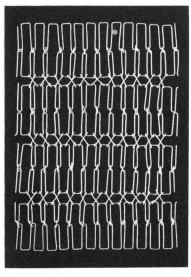

48 S

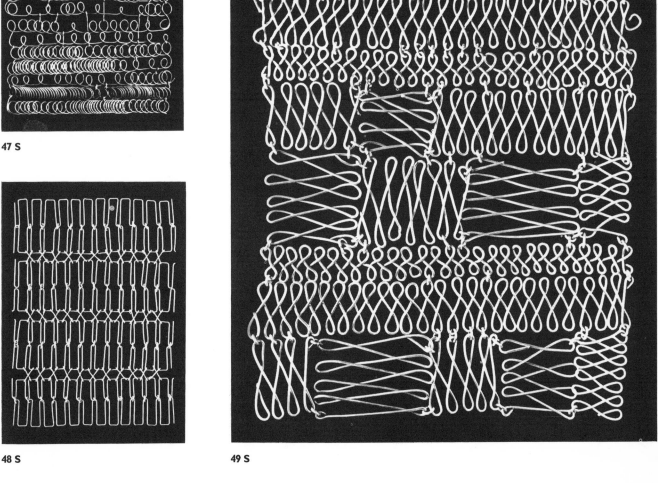

49 S

46, 48: Subdivision of a plane by angular wire shapes in free and in regular order.

47: Series of wire bands made of helical springs, some loose, some dense, partly overlapping.

49: Pendant of vertically and horizontally joined groups.

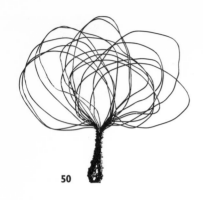

50

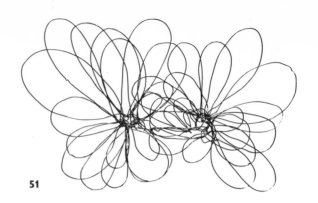

51

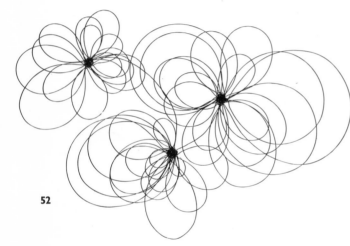

52

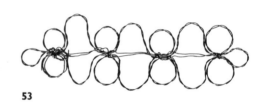

53

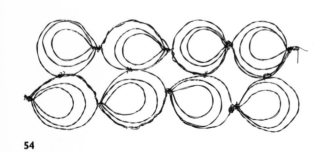

54

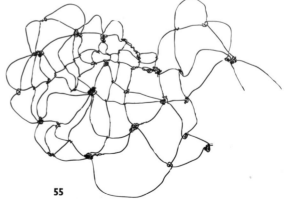

55

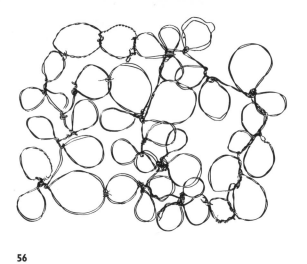

56

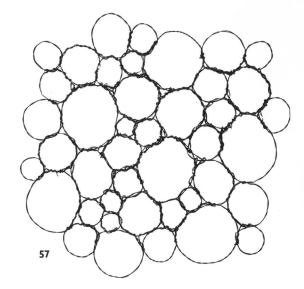

57

TYING AND TWISTING

Tying and twisting are among the more elementary methods of joining two or more ends of wire. These exercises were done by hand only. The materials are thin copper wire, 0.3 mm thick, soft and medium-hard.

50-52: 'Wire lines' may start from one or several points and return to them to be knotted or twisted. The elasticity of medium-hard wire produces tense shapes (52).

53-56: Two wires are twisted or corded together and form a base for round shapes, also twisted together.

55: Net-like structure with junctions in loose order. Soft material.

57: Cell-like formation with wide and narrow meshes.

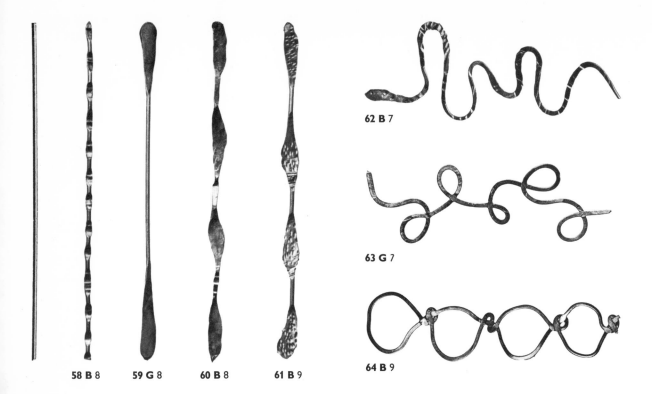

58 B 8   59 G 8   60 B 8   61 B 9

62 B 7

63 G 7

64 B 9

HAMMERING

Soft wire may be hammered on a steel base. Under the pressure of the hammer the wire flattens out. The denser parts become harder and more brittle. 71 and 72 illustrate the degree of malleability of a soft aluminium wire to the point of 'fraying'.

58-64: 'Forged' work by children using the head and claw of a hammer. Simple structures of hammered and untreated elements.

65-72: Play with 'cold-hammered' aluminium wire. Filed nails, punches and flat-nosed pliers were used as additional tools. Wire thicknesses: 1.5-2.5 mm.

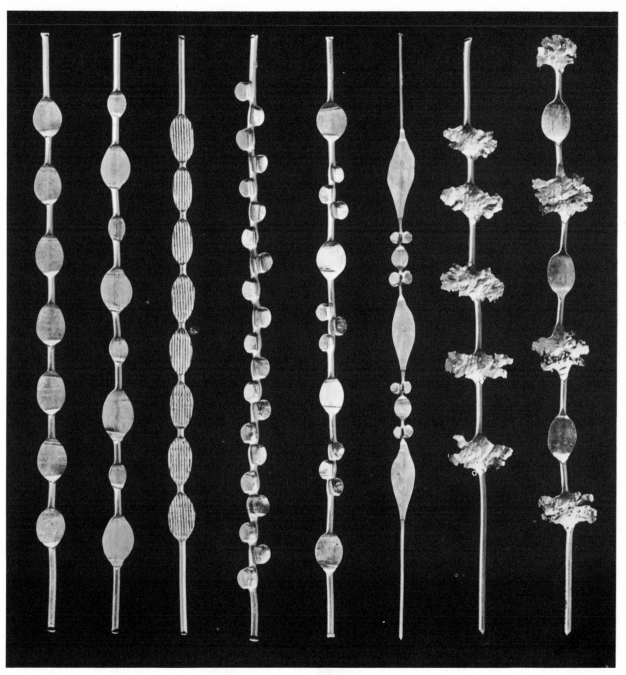

65   66   67   68   69   70   71   72

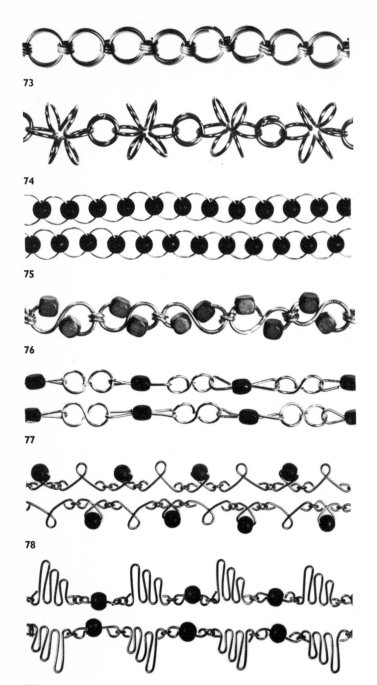

73

74

75

76

77

78

79

WIRE JEWELLERY

Chains consist of loosely joined links which should have clean outlines and be proportionate in size to the thickness of the wire. The chains illustrated here are easy to make, as they do not need soldering. The only tools required are a pair of small round-nosed pliers, flat-nosed pliers and a tin-snip. For circular links, the wire is wound round wooden or metal stakes. Single or multiple rings are cut off the resulting coil and used as basic elements (73-77, 81). Other shapes may be obtained by means of round or flat pliers or with a moulding stick (78-80, 82-84).

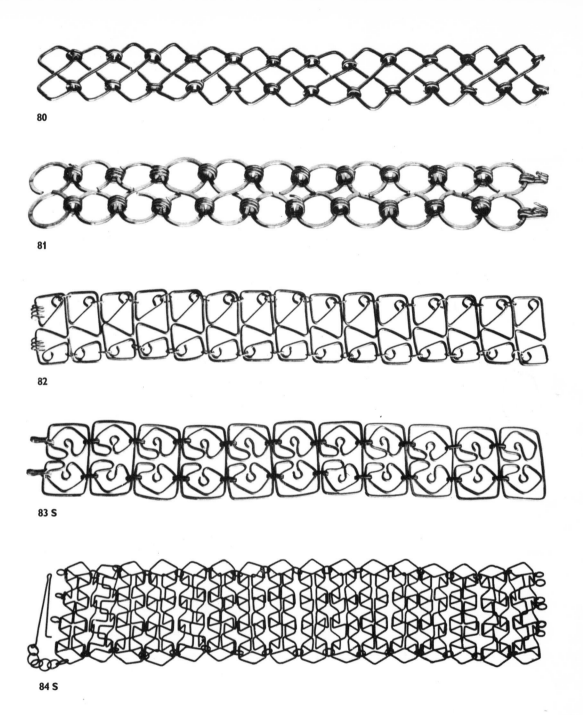

80

81

82

83 S

84 S

85

86

87

The examples shown on pages 10-15 are most important as preliminary exercises for wire jewellery. They help to develop an appreciation of the qualities of the material and to stimulate the imagination. Illustrations 85-92 show some further examples of wire jewellery.

88: Bracelet woven with the aid of a bending frame. The frame consists of a wooden platform into which an uneven number of nails are driven at short regular intervals to form a circle. The heads of the nails are then cut off. Thin wires (about 0.4 mm) are wound in and out round the nails to produce a kind of basket work. The bracelet is pulled off and wire threaded through the holes left by the nails.

91, 92: Thin wires no stronger than a thread can be crocheted. In 91, beads were incorporated in the loose structure. Material: soft copper wire, 0.2 mm thick.

88

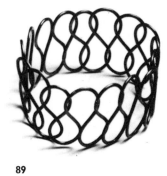

89

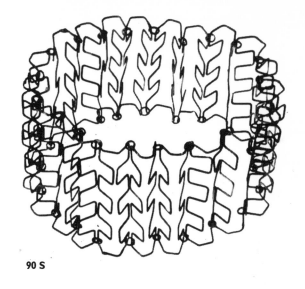

90 S

91 G 14

92

23

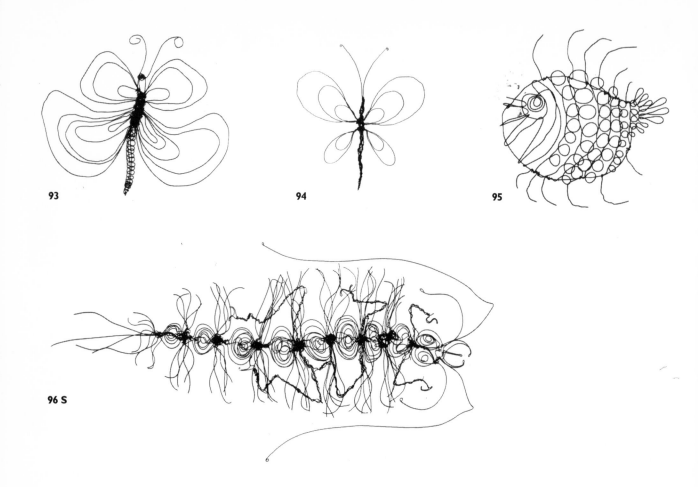

93

94

95

96 S

FIGURES

The linear character of wire permits the creation of 'wire drawings'. In 93-96, the wire, in accordance with its nature, expresses movement and direction, circumscribes planes and forms structures. The strands are joined by knotting, tying and twisting. Materials: annealed steel wire (binding wire) and galvanized steel wire, 0.6 mm thick.

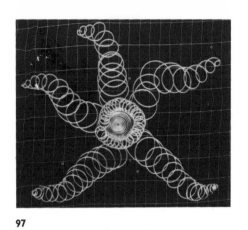

97

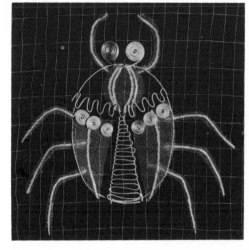

98

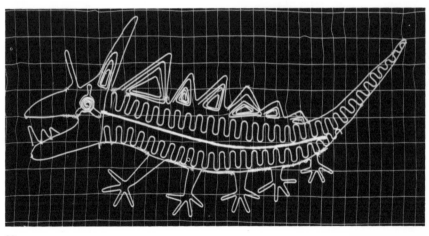

99

97-99: Animal figures of soft aluminium wire fastened to a lattice base of thin wire. The starfish consists of various spirals.

100

101

102

100, 101: The wire animals require a skeleton of soft binding wire. The curly, loosely formed bodies consist of helical springs.

102: A worm-like creature, entirely evolved from various kinds of wire. The body is elastic. When stretched, it springs back to its original shape.

103-106: The insect is a particularly suitable shape for figurative wire work, because wire is easily made to resemble its delicate body structure.

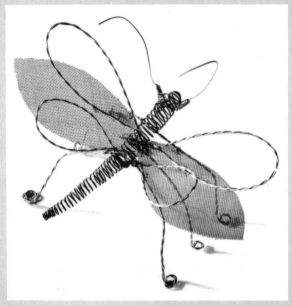

103

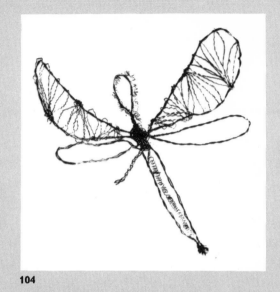

104

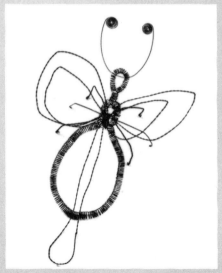

105

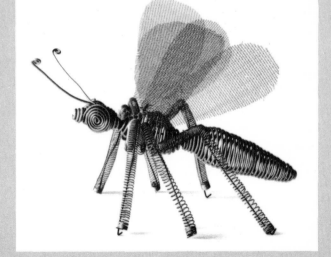

106

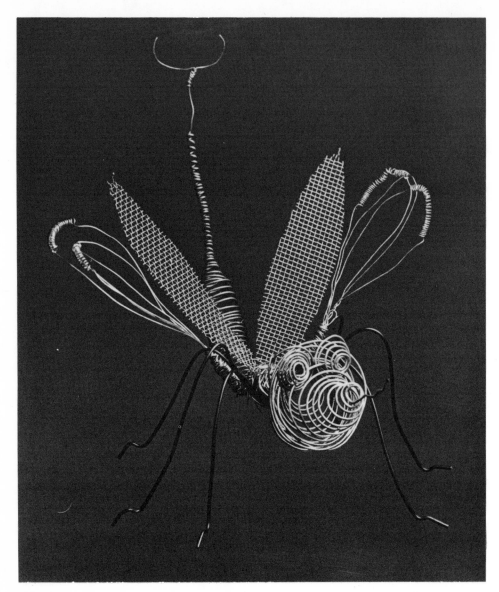

107

107: 'Aggressive Insect'.

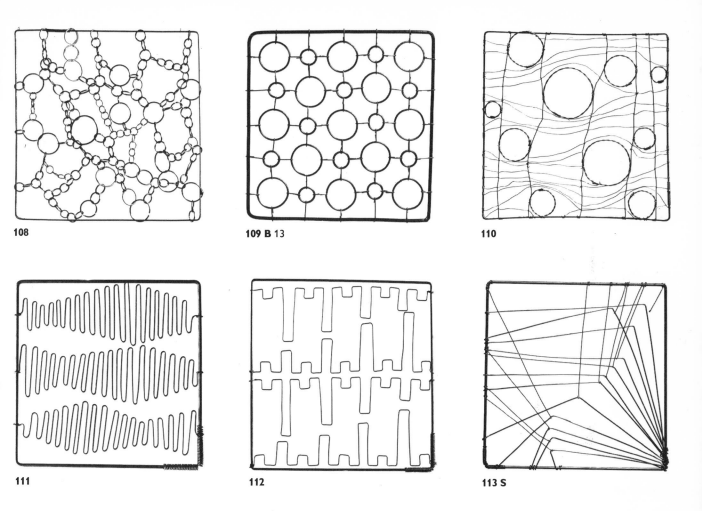

108

109 B 13

110

111

112

113 S

LATTICE WORK

In these exercises (108-116) a plane of a given size, surrounded by a wire frame, had to be filled with lattice work. The lattice is well known as a means of securing and defining spaces. In former times, artistic doors, gates and lattice work were made of wrought iron. Today they are usually machine-made.

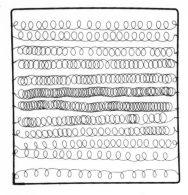

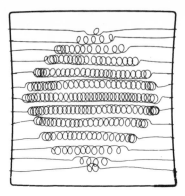

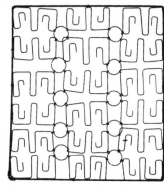

114 S   115 S   116 S

108-122 show lattice work which can be made without soldering. Here the basic forms are square and oblong planes framed by wire. The frames are of stronger wire bent at right angles, the two ends being joined by helical springs (see 111). The most suitable material for the frames is welded or galvanized wire which can be obtained in the shape of rods (about 2-3 mm thick).

The process of construction is directed by fixed rules. The basic figurative element is the three-dimensional line, which is capable of a great number of variations: it may be straight, curved, wavy, broken, irregular or intertwined; it may form a ring (108) or a spiral (119); it can be thickened or thinned by hammering (118, 121). 108, 109: The ring as a basic shape may form a loose net of chains (108) or a regular pattern (109). In 110, circular shapes are incorporated in the net-like structure.

111, 113: Subdivision of a surface by wavy and angular strung wires.

114, 115: Play with the lines of uncoiled springs.

116: Pattern of contrasting pairs (round-angular).

30

117 S

117: Line composition for two voices with variations on a basic theme.

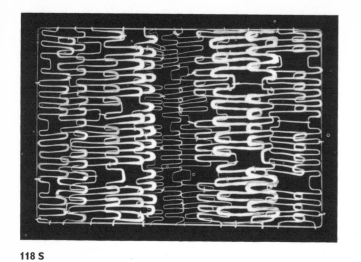

118 S

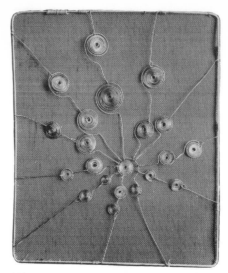

119

120

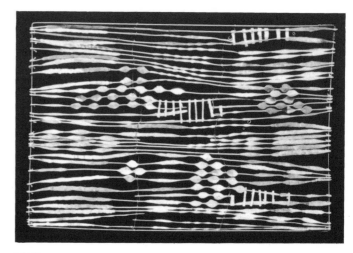

121 S

118, 121: Pattern of increasing and decreasing lines. The varying thickness of the wire is produced by hammering.

Material: soft aluminium wire, 1.2 mm thick.

119, 120: Patterns with spirals. The background consists of thin wire fabric.

32

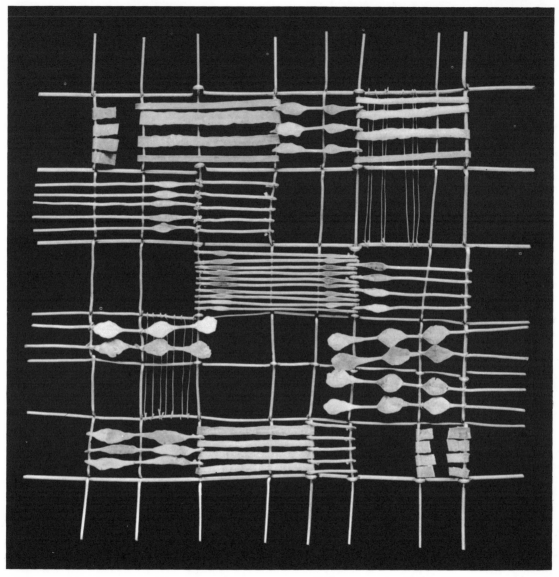

122 S

122: Lattice work of vertical and horizontal wires. Contrast between structures and unstructured planes.
Materials: hammered and unhammered aluminium wires.

33

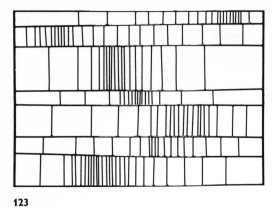

123

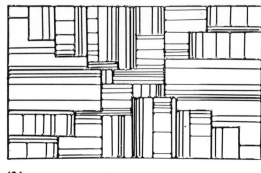

124

125

126 B 14

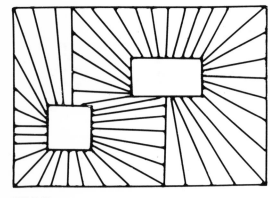

127 B 13

128

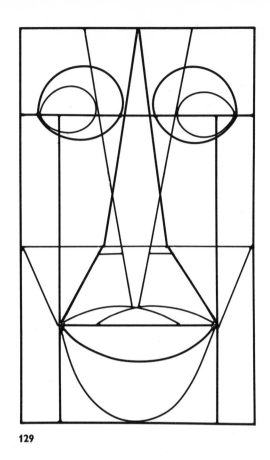

129

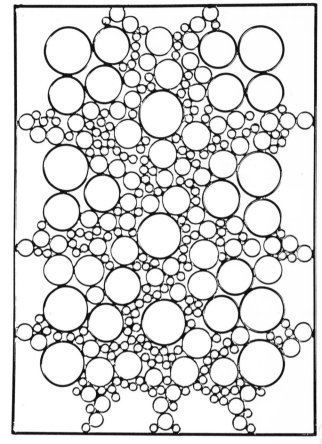

130 S

SOLDERED LATTICE WORK

Soldering offers a fresh variety of possibilities. 123-127 illustrate the progressive stages of a single development. In 123 and 124 the set task was to subdivide a plane by vertical and horizontal lines; in 125-127, to arrange two or three basic forms, circles, squares or oblongs, on a plane, making good use of the available space. These forms were to be joined by wires soldered to the frame.

128, 129: Figurative themes: 'Oriental Architecture' and 'Mask'.

130 shows an interesting rhythmical composition of circular elements.

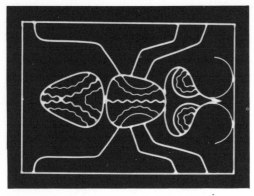

131

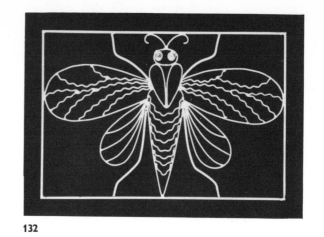

132

133 **B** 15

134

131-134: Insects and beetles: utilising the linear nature of wire. Soldered. Original size about 8″×12″.

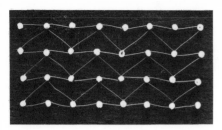

135 B 11

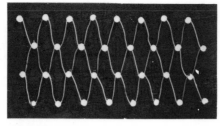

136 B 12

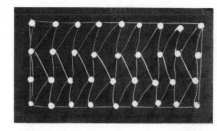

137 B 11

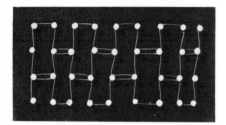

138 B 11

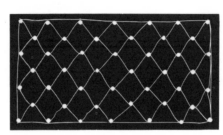

139 B 11

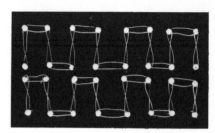

140 B 12

WIRE AND NAILS

Young children love to drive in nails and to string them together with wire. Wire, nails and waste pieces of hardboard or thin wooden board are required for these exercises. The method is very simple. A piece of squared or graph-paper is pinned to a dark board, so that the holes into which the nails are to be driven can be accurately marked out with a skewer or other pointed object. When the nails have been hammered in, the game of stringing wire round them may begin, the only condition being that the whole surface must be covered with a single, unbroken length of wire.

135-140 illustrate simple exercises with a developing pattern, from which more sophisticated patterns (144-146) are evolved.

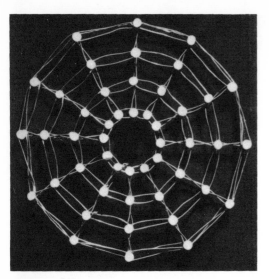

141 B 13

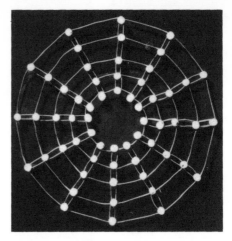

142 B 13

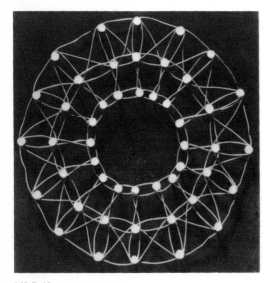

143 B 13

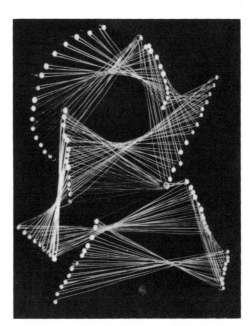

144 S

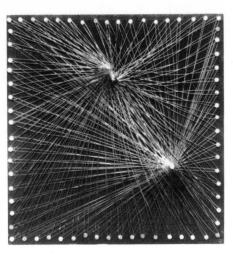

145 S

141: The circle as a starting point for stringing exercises.

144: Diagonally intersecting wires with a markedly dynamic effect.

145: Wires issuing from two focal points produce two interpenetrating 'magnetic fields'.

146: Free composition of point (nail head) and line (wire) as figurative elements.

146 S

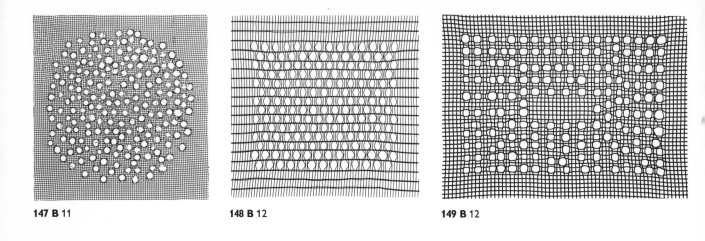

147 B 11   **148 B** 12   **149 B** 12

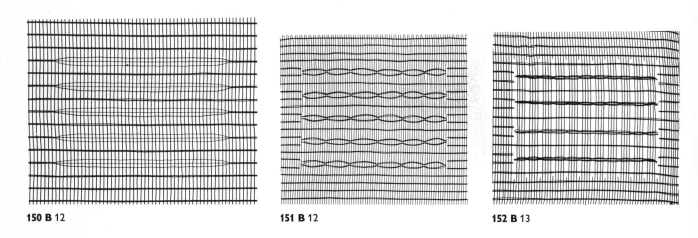

150 B 12   **151 B** 12   **152 B** 13

WORKING WITH FABRIC

PLANES

The structure of wire fabrics is similar to that of textiles. They consist of weft and warp which together form a connected whole. As always, we begin with simple exercises. Illustrations 147-159 show examples of different developments, in each of which the figurative problem was regarded as central. The structure of wire fabric may

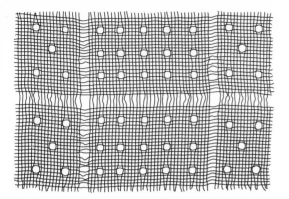

153 B 12

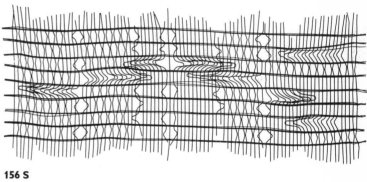

154

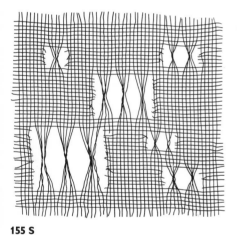

155 S

156 S

be altered by bending, shifting, pulling out or cutting the wires. 147-153 show examples in which the rectangular meshes were widened to circular or oval shapes by means of a pencil. In addition, in 153, some weft and warp wires were removed. Interesting structural alterations and fresh shapes may be obtained by cutting, shifting or bending the wires (150-152, 154-159).

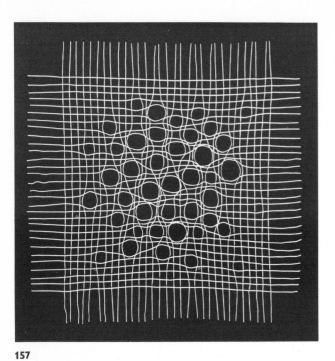

157

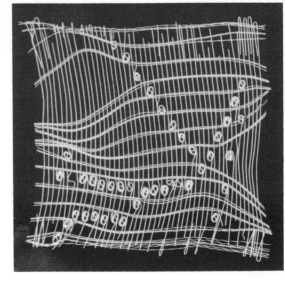

158 S

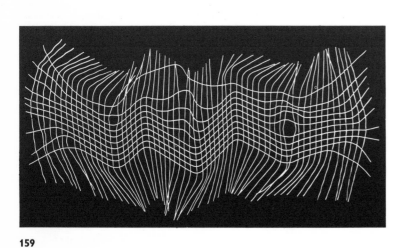

159

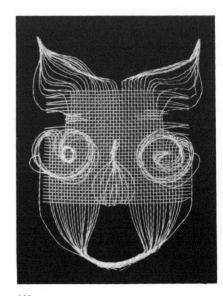

160

160: A mask of fabric formed by removing, shifting and bending wires.

42

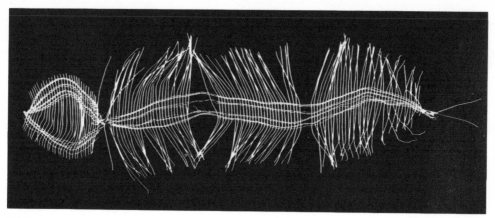

161 T

162

161, 162: Two objects of oblong pieces of fabric, resembling fossils.

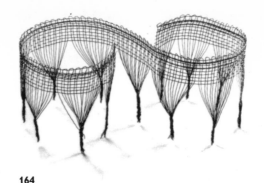

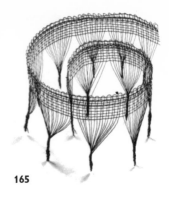

163

164

165

SPATIAL WORK

Wire fabric has the characteristics of structural planes. If bent, they form three-dimensional objects enclosing space or jutting out into space.

163-165: Three possibilities of spatial variations in a strip of fabric, the lower border of which was changed by removing some horizontal wires and twisting together the remaining strands. Despite the airy appearance, the supporting parts at the bottom seem to be bearing a load, and give the impression of standing.

166, 167: Alterations in a cylindrical form lead to apparently architectural objects. The two edges of the mantle are joined by thin wires.

168-171: Botanical shapes of oblong pieces of fabric. The vertical wires are removed except for the central spine, and the horizontal wires twisted and bent in all directions for spatial effect.

44

166

167

169

168

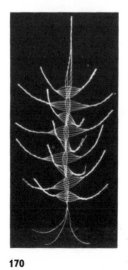

170

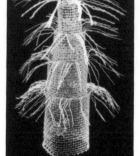

171

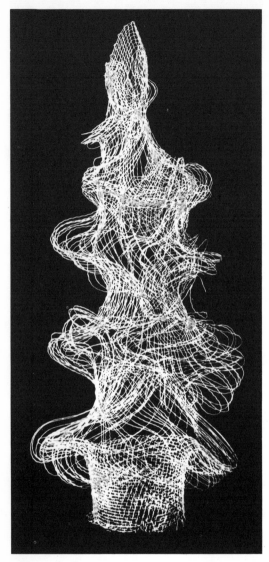

172

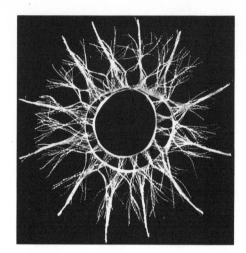

173

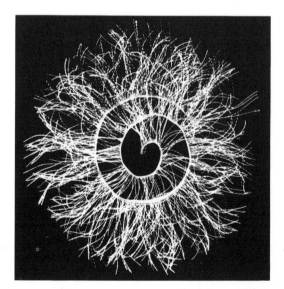

174

172: A twisted botanical shape evolved from a variation of the cylindrical form.

173, 174: Two spirals of oblong pieces of fabric. Vertical wires are removed, and the horizontal ones twirled and ruffled.

175 S

Wire fabrics may have very varying characteristics, depending on the size and shape of the mesh, the thickness of the wire, the colour of the metal, and the weave.

A very elastic fabric of small mesh and thin wire was used for 175. A length of rectangular wire fabric was to be rearranged by vertical and horizontal folds. As wire tends to get harder when strained and bent, the resulting fabric, unlike a piece of textile, becomes tougher.

176

177

178

These animal figures (176-178) of wire fabric reveal the peculiar charm of this material and its versatility. No soldering is required. The parts are held together by fine wires (see 177).

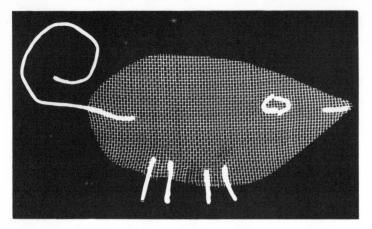

179 B 7

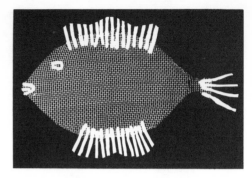

180 G 8

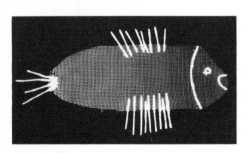

181 G 8

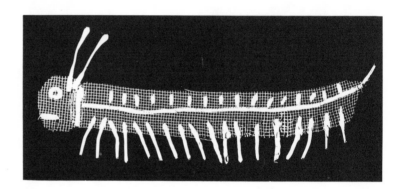

182 B 9

FABRIC AND WIRE

Soft aluminium wire can be hammered on to wire fabric. The hard wires of the fabric cut into the soft aluminium, and a firm connection results. The method is so simple that even younger children can use it.

179-182: Animal shapes cut from wire fabric with an old pair of scissors. The wire was hammered on subsequently.

183: 'Reptile'. Fabric with frayed edges and decorated with aluminium wire.

184: Spirals hammered on to fabric.

50

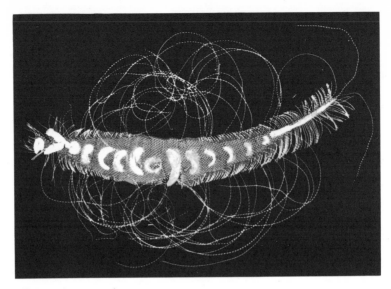

183 S

184

WORKING WITH TIN

EMBOSSING AND PUNCHING

Metals generally are available in a preformed state. Apart from preformed materials, such as wire and wire fabric, rolled tin is a most suitable medium for metal work. Its possibilities are endless. It may serve as a background to figurative patterns, lends itself to relief work and plane structures, and can be made into three-dimensional objects, e.g. by bending or chasing. Embossing and chasing are processes which require a malleable and resilient material, such as thin, soft plate of aluminium, copper, brass, zinc and tin. They cause plastic changes in the material. Placed on a soft pad and worked with chasing or embossing tools, the tin expands downwards to form raised dots, lines and planes. As the metal expands, it becomes harder and more brittle. Illustrations 185-193 show exercises with a plane structure. A variety of materials, methods and tools was used. In 185, 186, 188-190, soft aluminium foil was placed on a pad of folded newspaper. Round sticks of beech wood sharpened at one end were used as instruments. 187, 191-193 show work in soft copper and lead plate. In chasing, as distinct from embossing, the tool is driven by a hammer. The tool may be a nail of piece of welded wire (2 and 3 mm thick), hand-filed to various forms and sizes.

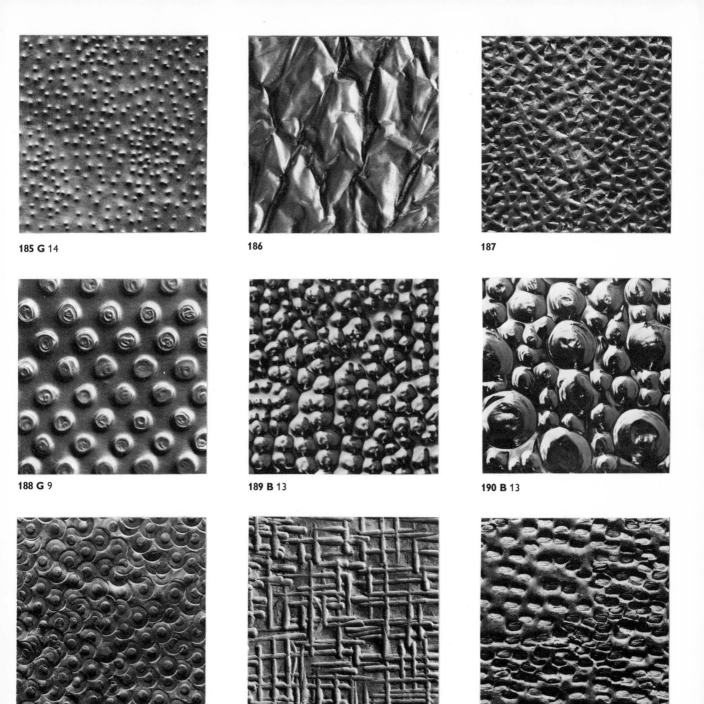

185 G 14

186

187

188 G 9

189 B 13

190 B 13

191

192

193

53

195 B 9

194 G 8

196 G 8

197

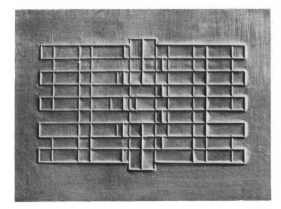

198

199

200 S

194-196: Animal forms embossed in soft aluminium foil with a ballpoint-pen or pencil. They show childrens' unerring instinct for form and material.

197-200: The raised line as an element of figurative order. 197-199: embossed into aluminium foil. 200: chased in lead plate.

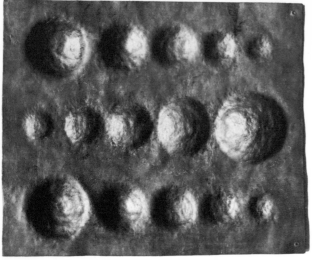

201 S

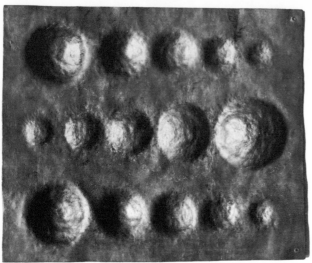

202 B 10

203 S

204 S

205

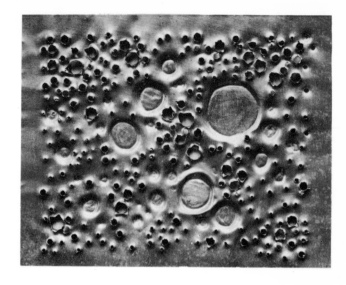

206

The softer and tougher the metals, the greater their malleability and plasticity. 202 shows the degree to which aluminium plate, 0.2 mm thick, may be beaten out of shape, in this case to produce a surface with larger and smaller indentations. The material was stretched to its utmost limit.

201: Pattern of convex and concave shapes in motion and counter-motion.

203: Squares repeated across a surface.

204: Circular composition of convex and concave, or positive and negative, shapes.

205, 206: In these exercises the tin has been punched as well as subjected to other processes. A pattern of small and large punctures in groups is shown in 205. In 206 a group of large depressions forms a contrast to small punctures.

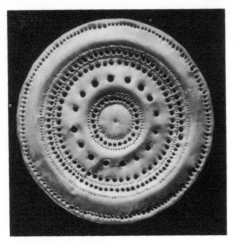

207

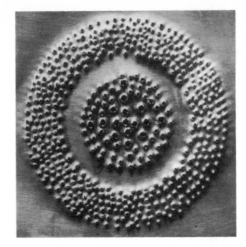

208 **B** 12

209 **B** 13

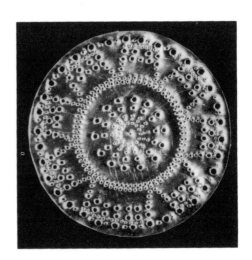

210

Punctures serve to break the heavy, solid effect of a surface, or to achieve constructive connections (rivets, screws). In these exercises (207-218) they have an ornamental effect. As a formal element, the hole or puncture

211 B 13   212 B 12   213 B 13

has the character of a dot. With thin tin or foil, the punching may be done on a soft pad.

The points of compasses, nails or other pointed objects may be used as tools. Round the edges of the puncture the material is forcibly deformed. Weals and ridges appear on the reverse side.

207-210: Larger and smaller punctures form a pattern on a circular surface.

211-213: Aluminium foil bent to form a hollow cylinder. The two edges are joined by adhesive. The reflection of the light on the shiny metal produces a particularly charming effect. Lanterns can be made in the same way.

214 G 8

215 B 9

216 B 9

217 B 11

214-217: Punched animal shapes of soft aluminium foil (0.2 mm thick). The shapes were subsequently cut out with old scissors.

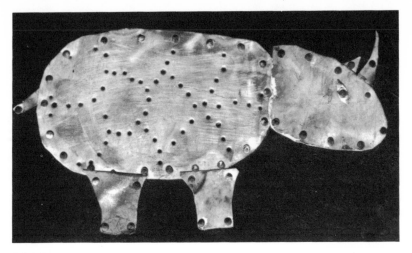

218 B12

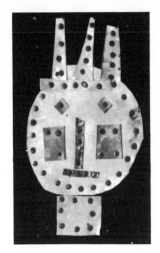

219 B 9

ASSEMBLING AND MOUNTING WITH NAILS AND WIRE

By assembling we mean the jointing together of separate parts into a connected whole. The best material is thin tin, especially tin plate, which is easily cut with a pair of goldsmith's scissors. The following examples (218-232) show assembled relief and plane figures. The background consists of either a dark wooden board (hardboard or plywood) or wire fabric.

218-220: Figurative work, partly punched and mounted on hardboard. The nail heads have an ornamental effect.

220 B 14

61

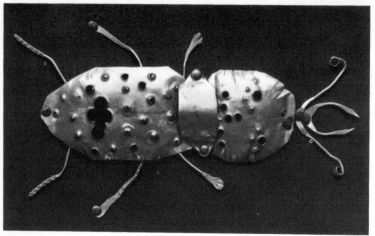

221 B 11

222 B 6

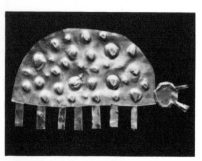

223 G 6

224 B 11

221, 224: Two beetles designed by a boy of 11. These exercises are useful for gaining experience of form and material such as tin and wire.

222, 223: Ladybirds made by first-year schoolchildren and stuck on boards with adhesive.

225 B 14

226 B 14

227 B 14

228 B 14

225-228: Schoolboys are always interested in mechanical things. The subject 'motor car' was chosen not only from a functional but also from a figurative point of view. Punched pieces of tin plate nailed on boards.

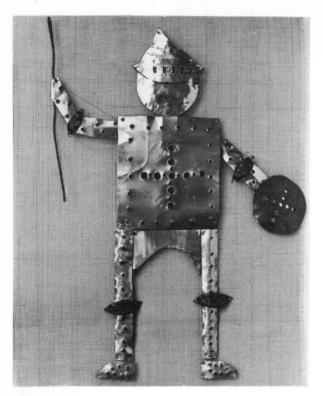

229 B 11

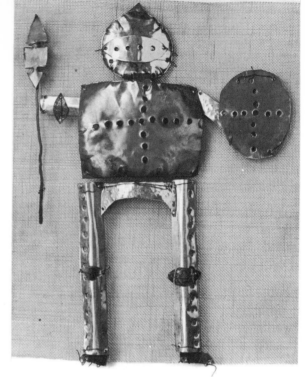

230 B 11

229, 230: The subject 'knight in armour' challenges a child's ability to work with metal and is well within the interest and experience of 11-year-olds. The figurative order is dictated by the material (tin), the process of assembly and the required tools. The separate parts which go to make up the figure had to correspond to the basic forms of square, oblong, circle and oval. Some parts were beaten out (230) and further divided and patterned by punching. The figures were mounted on wire fabric by means of thin wires. Tins and foils of different colours provide an additional interest, which may be further enhanced by gently heating the tin with a soldering iron to produce a 'tarnish'.

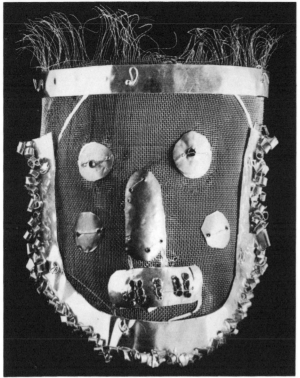

231 B 12

232 B 12

231: The subject 'mask' offers interesting possibilities in metal work and especially in assembly. In this case the pupil mounted tin plate on wire fabric. The holes which take the mounting wires also serve an ornamental purpose. The tense expression results from the contrast between the smooth, shiny tin and the dull background of fabric.

232: Surface and line combine to give a figurative effect. The outlines of the face, mouth, nose and eyes consist of soft aluminium wire hammered on to the fabric. A punched crown, cut out of thin brass plate, frames the face at the top.

233

235

234

233: The shape of a jellyfish appears as a figure on a structured surface. It rises from a plain background and thus requires no outlines. Process: combination of embossing and punching.

234: Starfish punched into copper plate by means of two nails of different thicknesses. The points were filed to a spherical shape. The metal was darkened and the raised parts subsequently polished. Material: copper plate, 0.6 mm thick.

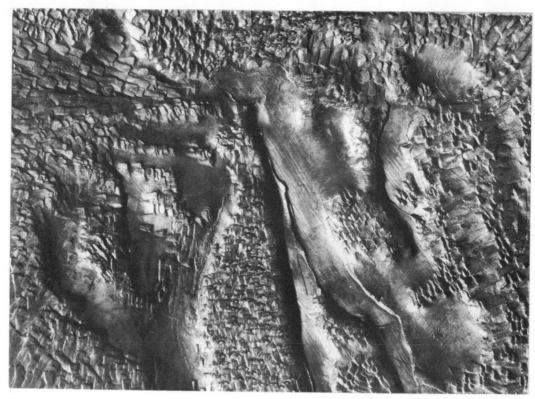

236 S

CHASING

Essentially the process is similar to that of embossing and punching. On a pad softer than the metal, the material is extended and pushed out of shape. The appropriate tools for larger protuberances are plastic hammers and hammers with ball heads: for smaller bosses, round sticks of hardwood. Aluminium plate and lead plate are very soft and malleable materials, as shown in 235 and 239. The animal shapes, 237-239, were chased on a soft pad as hollow figures.

237

238

239

240

VESSELS

There are two ways of forming a piece of tinplate into a vessel: raising and coursing. The bowls in 240 were raised. A cut-out, circular piece of metal is placed on a wood block hollowed out on its end grain. The metal is beaten with a round-nosed hammer, working from the centre outwards in spiral-form. As the metal becomes harder and more brittle in the process of stretching, it must be annealed and pickled after each completed round with the hammer. Raising extends the sides and bottom of the vessel, while the rim remains almost unchanged.

The prototype of a shallow bowl is the cupped hand. It is important that bottom and sides should have clear lines and be well proportioned in relation to each other. Material: soft copper plate, 0.8 mm thick.

241

242 S

243

244 S

245 S

Coursing (see technical tips p. 116) is another method of shaping tin into hollow vessels. It forces the metal worker to adopt simple forms and confine himself to essentials. All parts of the vessel, i.e. bottom, sides and opening, should be well-proportioned in size and form. The walls merit special attention. They may be slightly concave (241, left), or splay out in a straight line (242), or they may curve (243, 244). In the tumbler (centre of 241), the curve of the upper half forms a tense contrast to the straight line of the lower half. Further possibilities are shown in 244 and 245.

241: Tumblers in copper plate, 0.8 mm thick.

242: The rim of the tumbler on the left was further decorated by means of a chisel.

243: The natural traces of the planishing hammer and staining enliven the surface.

244: The enamelled rim lends an additional colour and form accent to the vessel.

245: A coursed vessel of silver tin, subsequently planished and polished.

246

247

248

249

250

Among the vessels that may be made of metal are boxes and cubical receptacles. The objects illustrated here were made with the aid of a blowpipe. Unlike the raised and coursed vessels made of one piece of tin, these have to be assembled and the various parts, i.e. bottom, sides, lid, joined together.

246: A napkin ring, partly embossed.

247: The tin sides of these vessels were bent round pipe sections and joined with a blow-pipe. Material: soft copper plate, 1.2 mm thick.

248: Boxes with lids, partly stained dark.

249, 250: Boxes of brass and copper plate, lids coloured.

251 B 10   252 B 11   253 B 11   254 B 10   255

BENDING AND CUTTING

Intensive work with tin demands methodical exercises. 251-257 show the steps of one such development, beginning with a simple exercise and ending with more sophisticated work. The basic element is a rectangular strip of tin cut with a pair of goldsmith's scissors.

251-253: Cuts at regular intervals down one side. Cuts at irregular intervals and resulting tongues of metal bent in different directions. Material: welded tin, 0.23 mm thick.

254, 255: The strip has been cut on both sides. The natural curling of the tin was accentuated and further developed by bending and rolling.

256, 257: Interesting three-dimensional objects, evolved from the nature of the material and its reaction to cutting.

256

257

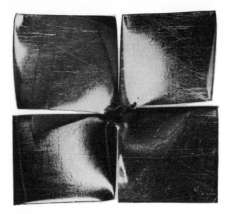

258 B 10

259 B 11

Tin has a 'grain' like paper. It is produced by rollers and thus stretched in one direction. In consequence, tin is harder to bend in the direction in which it was stretched. This is one of the lessons to be learned from playing with the material, shaping it and discovering its qualities. Another peculiarity appears when tin is cut with scissors. The edges to the right and left of the cut bend, one upwards and the other downwards. The basic material for the exercises illustrated here (258-263) is a piece of welded tin about 4″ square.

258, 259: The tin is cut horizontally, vertically and diagonally. When cut at right angles to the edges, the metal turns downwards on the right and upwards on the left (258), thus producing spatial forms.

260-263: In making narrow cuts along the edge, the scissors press the tin upwards and downwards, according to the position of the metal (263). In the four examples, the possibility of changing the direction of the bend is intentionally utilised to provide a regular pattern.

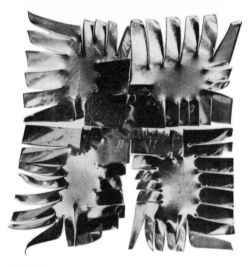

260 B 11

261 B 10

262 B 11

263 B 11

77

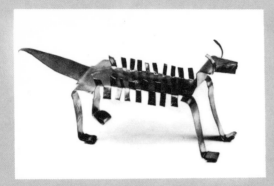

264 G 12

265 B 11

266

267

The experience gained in the previous exercises is bearing fruit in these figures (264-267). It is important at this point that play should be directed towards a particular purpose. In these examples, the players were asked to use a pair of goldsmith's scissors on an oblong piece of tin in such a way that none of the material was cut off, and to bend the cut strips into spatial figures.

264: At the start, the narrow edge of the tin (about $2^1/_2'' \times 7''$) was cut into strips of equal size, which were bent down to form the legs. The remaining strip between the legs formed head and tail. Small cuts along the long edge, alternatively bent up and down, produced the pattern of the body.

265: The task here was to form a reptile by diagonal cuts along the long edge.

266: The uniform structure is mainly due to the fact that the tin was cut lengthways only. The material was subsequently slightly tinted by means of a blowlamp.

267: Plastic animal figure with a lively expression, formed from a flat piece of tin.

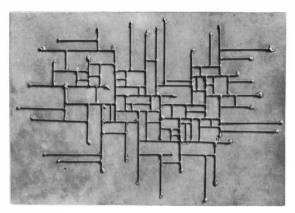

268 S

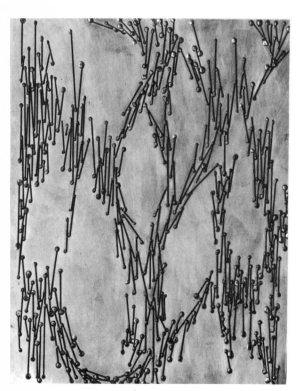

269 S

SOLDERED AND RIVETED RELIEF WORK

Wire soldered on to a background of tin achieves the effect of a flat relief (268), which may be heightened by using several wires on top of one another (271).

268: Pattern formed by vertical and horizontal wires. The composition is determined by the dense pattern at the centre dissolving towards the edges.

269: Short pieces of wire form the structural elements of rhythmical movement. The empty spaces are shaped. The soldering marks are intentionally employed as a figurative element (dot).

270: Closely placed wires form a pathway.

271: Spatial pattern of several wires soldered on top of one another.

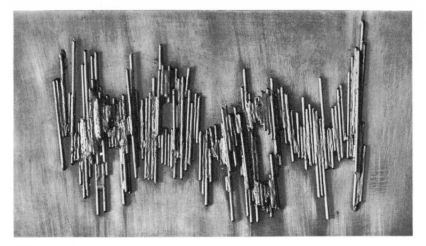

270 S

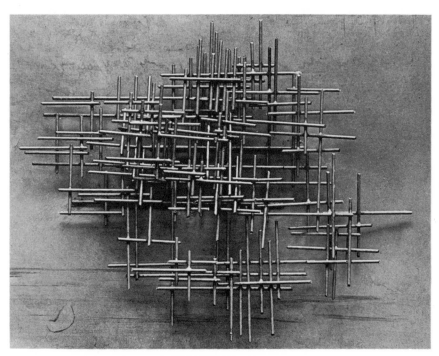

271 S

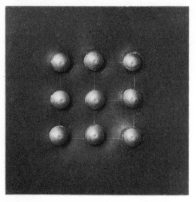

272 T

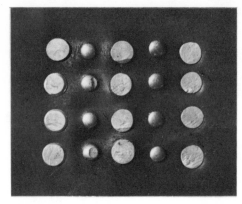

273 T

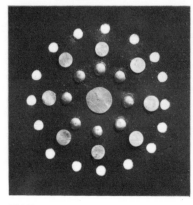

274 T

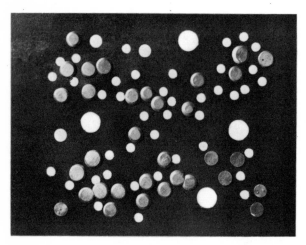

275 T

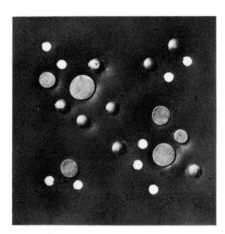

276 T

Riveting is essentially a method of firmly joining two pieces of metal. In these examples (272-276) the function of the rivets is purely decorative. The effect is that of dots. The rivet heads are hammered into flat surfaces.

272, 273: Orderly pattern. In 273, some of the rivets have been beaten flat.

274: Circular pattern. The dots consist of holes, rivet heads and flattened rivet heads.

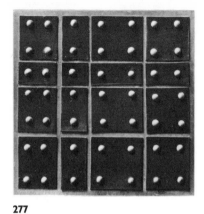

277

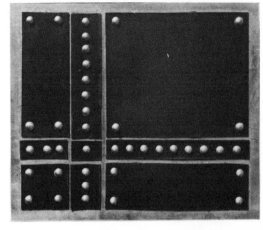

278

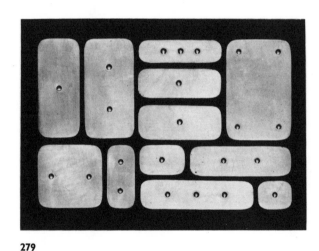

279

280

275, 276: Scattered pattern with some focal points. Contrasting sizes of holes and rivet heads.

277-280: In these examples the rivet serves a functional as well as a decorative purpose. A sheet of metal was to be cut into rectangular pieces which were bolted to a flat surface by rivets in a pattern of dots. The spaces between the pieces appear as lines.

281

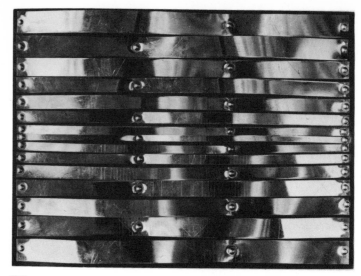

282

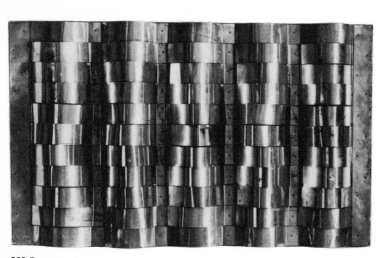

283 S

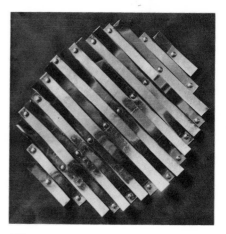

284

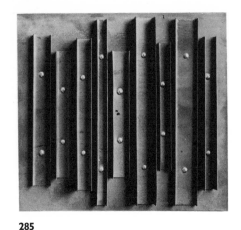

285

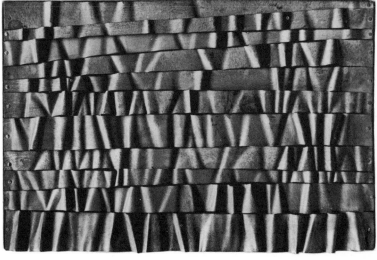

286

The basic material for these examples (281-289) was strips of welded tin or sheet iron. Their ribbon-like form expresses direction and movement. They may be arranged horizontally, vertically or diagonally, and offer many figurative possibilities. They may be bent, angled, folded and shaped to assume various profiles.

281: Vertical pattern of concave strips of tin. Motion in opposite directions.

282: Horizontal arrangement of curved strips. Flowing motion towards the centre.

283: Strong rhythmical movement. The strips are nailed to a wooden board.

284: Alternating convex and concave strips. The diagonal appearance of the pattern has a dynamic effect.

285: Strips of thin sheet iron were angled in U-form and riveted to a flat surface.

286: Folded ribbons of welded tin, slightly tinted by heating with a blow lamp.

287 S

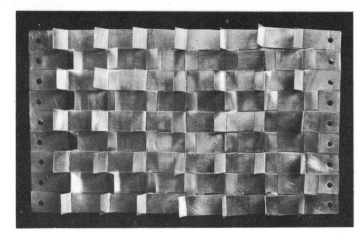

288

289 S

290

291

292 S

Welded tin reflects the light. Bend it, and the reflection is broken, the differences between dark and light areas being considerable. The lively play of light and shade becomes an essential part of the pattern.

287: Rhythmically patterned relief of triangular pieces which are soldered together.

288: Angled pieces of tin fixed with nails in a spatial order. The play of light and shade is due to the angled parts.

289: Two groups of folded strips in tense relation to each other.

290: Overlapping big and small circular shapes.

291: Box-shaped pieces fitted into one another to form a shallow spatial object.

292: A good instance of a convincing solution achieved by restriction to one basic element. Material: welded tin, 0.23 mm thick.

293 S

294 S

As in the earlier relief work, only one element was used in these examples (293-295). Set rules determined material, method, starting point and basic principles.

293: Pieces of welded tin bent into semicylindrical shapes round a wooden stick form the elements of this organically mobile relief.

294: Angled pieces of varying sizes were soldered together to form this cell-like formation. There is an effective contrast between the smaller pieces in the central zone and the larger ones at the edges.

295 S

295: This relief work is overlaid by a delicate play of light and shade. The numerous chiaroscuro nuances give the impression of swinging motion and facetted surfaces. An example of the strong reflection of light on shiny welded tin. The basic elements were strips of different widths, angled by means of pliers. Arranged in symmetrical order, they produce an interesting relief composition.

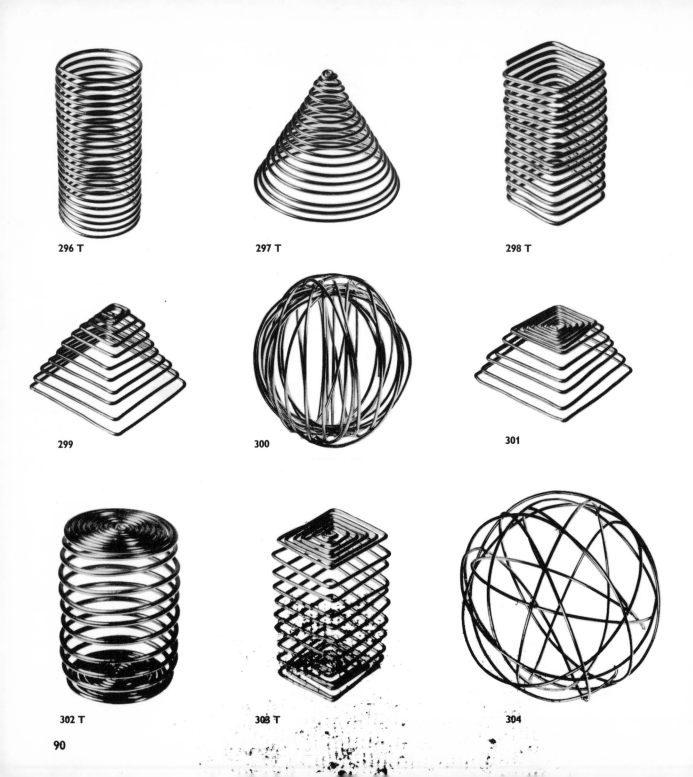

296 T   297 T   298 T

299   300   301

302 T   303 T   304

90

305

306 T

CONSTRUCTIVE SPATIAL WORK

WIRE

In constructive spatial work, wire offers many possibilities. Due to its rigidity, it can be made to jut out into space or to outline space. The initial exercises are confined to simple basic shapes and their variations. The examples represent a progressive series designed to inspire further development. Material: aluminium wire, 1.5 and 2 mm thick.

296, 302: A winding spiral encloses cylindrical space. It may begin and end with a flat spiral.

297, 299, 301: Cone, square-base and square-top pyramids as basic shapes.

298, 303: The ashlar is an elementary shape in building. Its vertical direction has a static effect. Spatial shapes of wire are transparent, their interior and back being equally visible.

300, 304-306: The sphere as a basic plastic shape, and its variations.

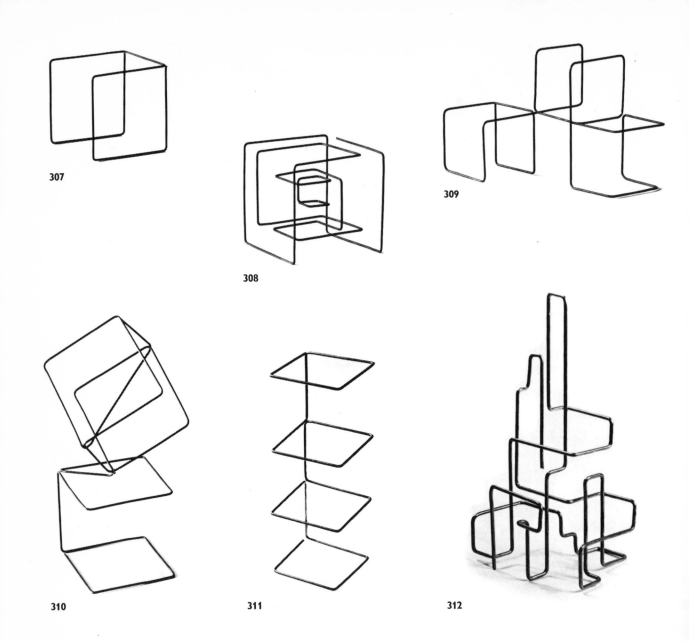

307, 308: From the first exercise, i.e. to make a cube of wire, evolves the second, i.e. to subdivide the interior space (308).

92

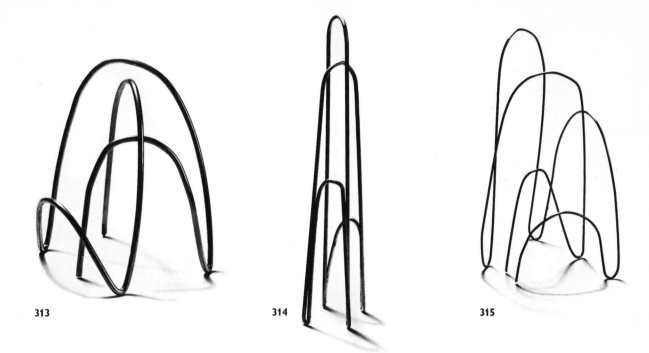

313

314

315

309: To shape a continuous length of wire into several cubes.

310: The tension in this composition of wire is due to the contrast between repose and motion. One edge of a cube balances on another which rests on the ground.

311: A spatial composition of several surfaces, one above the other.

312: Here the task was to pull out a continuous length of wire to form a balanced entity, the wire always to run straight and any change of direction to be contrived by means of a right angle. Material: soft aluminium wire, 1.5 mm thick.

313-315: A curved wire shape. Space is contained between rising and falling movements.

316

317

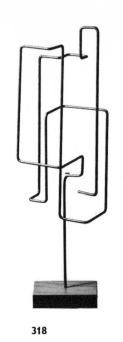

318

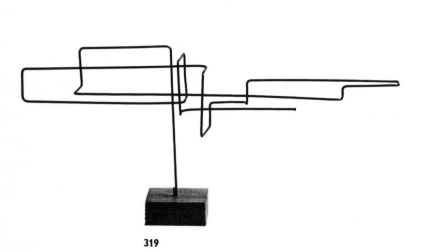

319

320

94

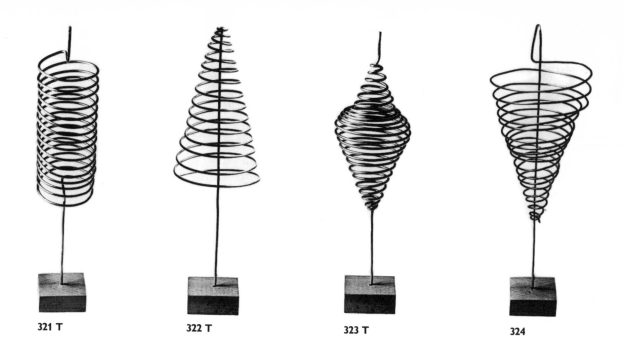

321 T 322 T 323 T 324

A plastic shape appears lighter when it is lifted off the ground and seems to float in space. In the preceding examples, the figures rested immediately on the ground. In these examples the centre of gravity is at the top.

316: Cubic empty space activated and divided from the surrounding space by wire. Material: rods of welded wire, 1.5 mm thick.

318, 319: Similar exercises, except that the cubic space was to be subdivided by horizontal and vertical lines.

317, 320: The wire changes direction at an acute angle. This results in triangular shapes jutting out into space on all sides.

321: A helical spring, bent round a stick, appears lighter when it is lifted off the ground.

322-324: Spiral shapes, terminating in a cone at the upper (322) and at the lower (324) end. In 323 the regular spindle shape has been varied by a slight depression of the upper part.

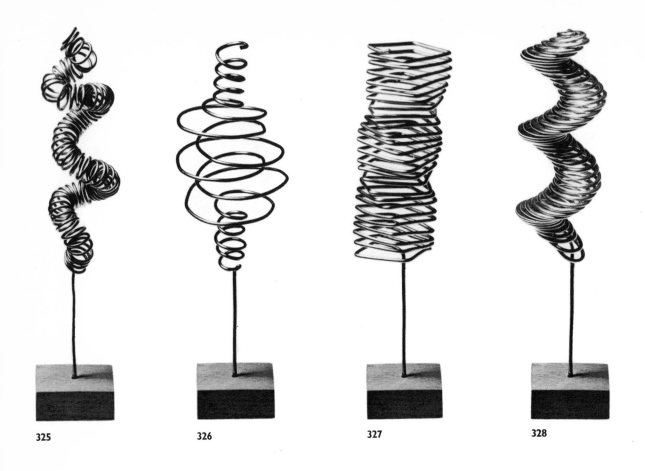

325   326   327   328

In contrast to 316-324, which are of a mainly static character, these figures are emphatically dynamic. The theme of these exercises was a spiral winding into space.

325, 328: Spiralling spirals.

326: An effective contrast between close and loose spirals.

327: Twisting gives the effect of a counter-movement in this spiral which was wound round a four-sided stick.

329-331: Further variations on the theme of 'floating spirals and spheres of wire'.

96

329 T

330

331

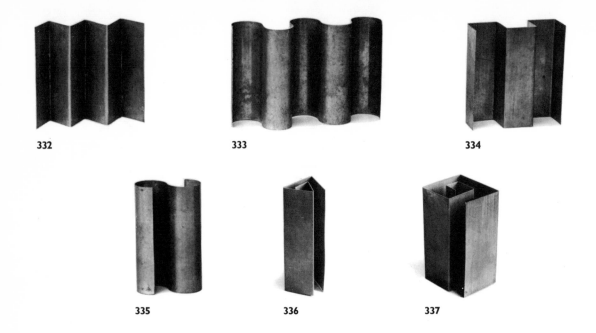

332   333   334

335   336   337

TIN

For constructive spatial work in tin it is best to begin with simple bending exercises. We examine the various possibilities of dividing up the flat pieces of tin. Several tools and aids are required. The tin is angled by means of hardwood stakes or bending bars (one flat, one with a square cross-section) firmly held. The tin is bent with a wooden mallet or plastic hammer. A special bench is required for angling longer pieces of tin. In order to achieve the cylindrical shape, the tin is bent round strong stakes or pipe sections. 338-343 were mostly worked from a single piece of tin.

322-337: Elementary forms of round and angled pieces of tin.

338: Groups of similar elements forming a unit. Material: sheet iron, 0.4 mm thick.

339-342: Pieces of tin cut and bent into spatial shapes; angular in 339, 340, and 342; soft and round in 341.

338

339

340

341

342 S

99

343

343: An oblong piece of tin is cut along both long edges at regular intervals. The resulting strips are angled by means of flat pliers to enclose rectangular space. A constructive spatial figure of regularly repeated features.

TIN, WIRE AND FABRIC

344: Steel spring wire is very elastic. When it is bent, the effect is one of tension. In this exercise the base is of punched tin. The size of the holes corresponds to the thickness of the wire (1 mm) which is slotted in and soldered. Wires of different curvatures enclose interpenetrating spaces.

345: Combination of wire and fabric. Wire rods of 1 mm thickness form a scaffold consisting of two vertical elements connected by horizontal wires. The open cubic spaces which result from the use of vertical and horizontal lines only are partly filled with fabric.

346: The interesting effect of this work is due to the contrast between the light sections, where the fabric is single, and the dark ones, where two pieces overlap and new shapes appear.

347: Spatial order and interpenetration in a symmetrical composition. Material: punched tin and hard spring wire, cold-soldered.

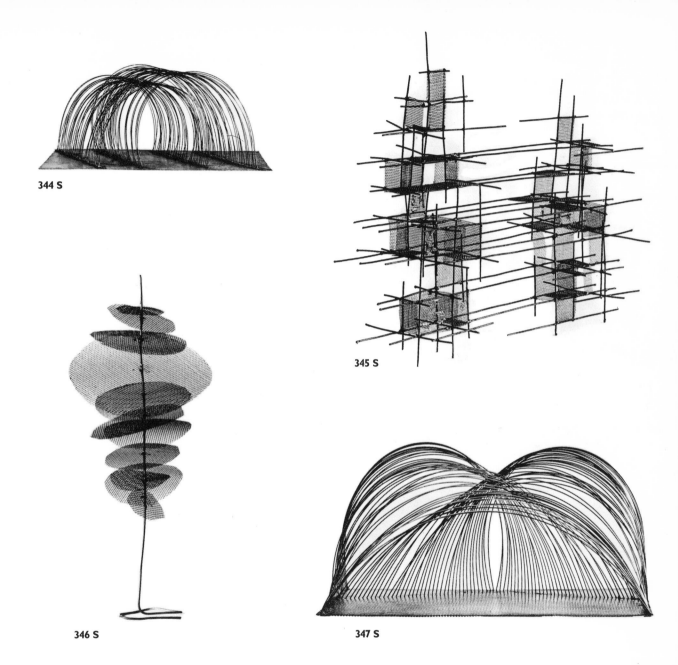

344 S

345 S

346 S

347 S

348 S

348: The contrast between line and surface, wire and fabric, produces a tense effect. The wires are grouped according to length in a vertical direction and related to the apparently floating pieces of fabric.

349, 350: The basic form is a cube outlined by wire. The task was to subdivide the interior space and thus to activate it. This may be done in various ways. In this example, the rules demanded two or more focal points to be joined to the edges of the cube.

351: Here the interior space of the cube is divided into smaller cubes with interpenetrating spaces in between.

352: Diagonal wires inside the cube result in parabola-shaped surfaces. The special charm of this work lies in the fact that the shape changes with different points of view.

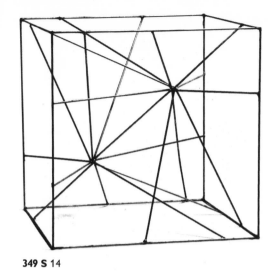

349 S 14

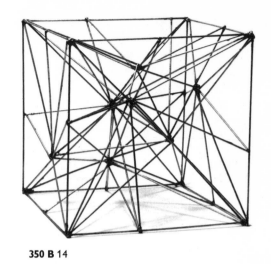

350 B 14

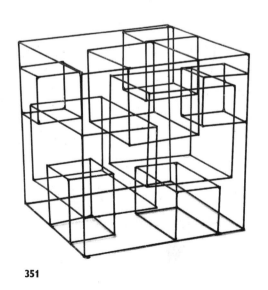

351

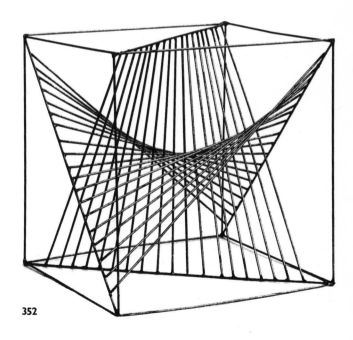

352

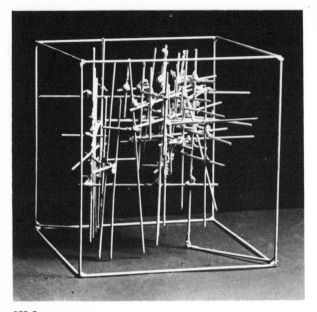

353 S

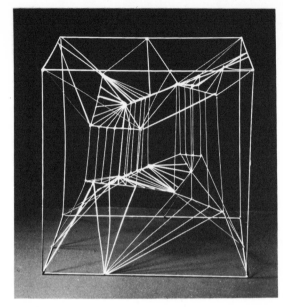

354 S

353: The cube encloses an object of densely intersecting wires which has a massive effect and by its independent shape creates visible tension. The solder forms little knobs to underline the figurative intention. Material: galvanized rods of steel wire, 1.5 mm thick.

354: In contrast to 355, in this construction the shapes in the interior are joined to the edges of the cube. Weight and density in 353 dissolve into weightlessness and transparence.

The play with cubes is especially fruitful in acquiring knowledge of the laws of space.

355: A particularly effective solution.

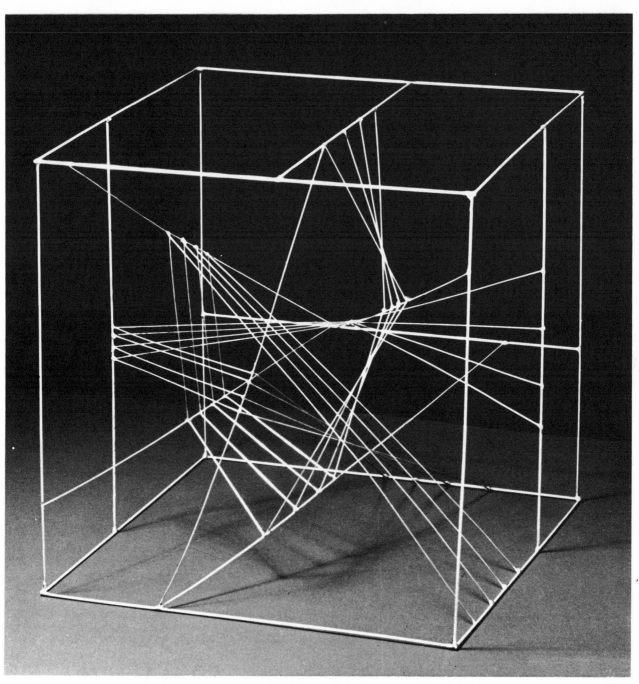

355 S

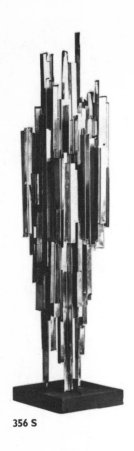

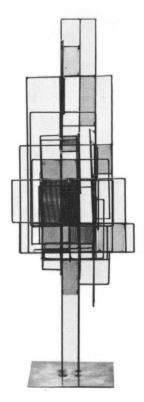

356 S   357 S   358 S

356: The basic element for this exercise is the T-square of welded tin. It is very suitable for constructive spatial work. Height, about 24″, soldered.

357: Vegetable or fruit tins are useful waste material. The cylindrical form of the tin is developed into a plastic object with vertical and horizontal elements. Soldered.

358: Constructive geometrical form of wire and wire fabric with plane effects.

359: Combination of wire with pieces of tin. The vertical composition of perpendicular and horizontal elements, open on all sides, has its focal point in the centre.

360: Wire fabric bent into plastic shapes and soldered. An interesting composition of closed and open fabric shapes.

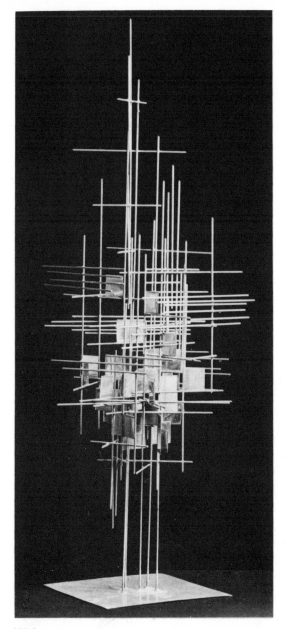

359 S

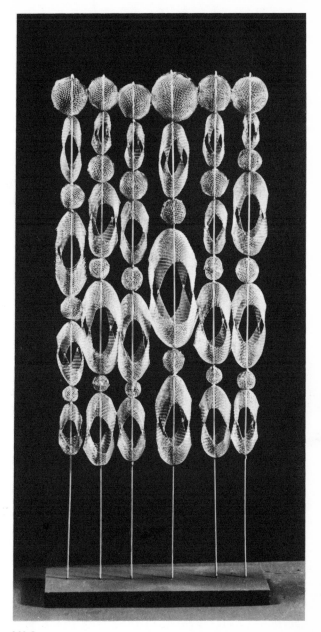

360 S

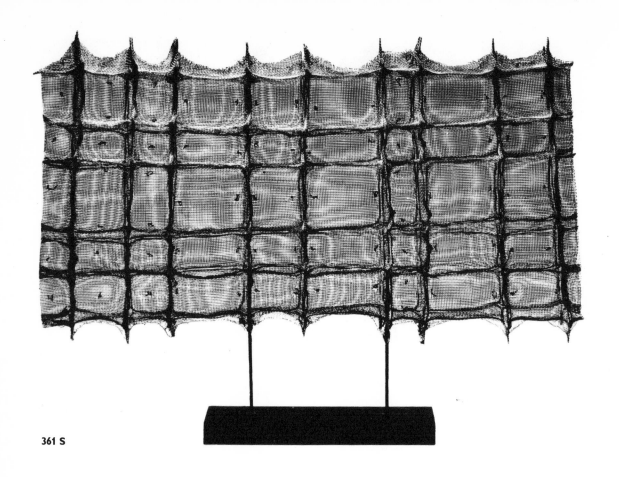

361 S

361: The sieve-like, transparent character of wire fabric has its own peculiar charm, especially when two overlapping pieces produce a shot-silk effect. Where the fabric is folded it appears darker. The linear effect in this example was achieved by folding. The dotted soldering points enhance the figurative effect.

362: A surprisingly rich and differentiated grouping of wires with sensitively expressed changes of direction.

362 S

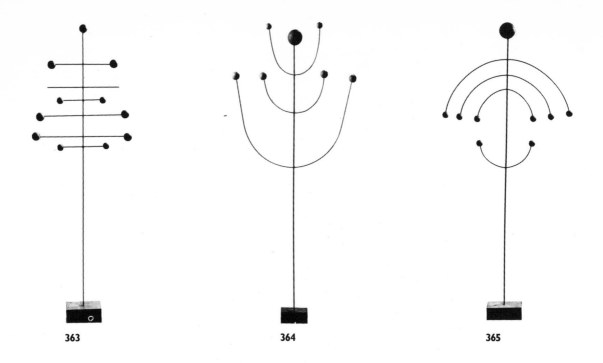

363   364   365

CONSTRUCTIVE DYNAMIC WORK

VIBRATION, PENDULUM AND GEARS

These examples from the sphere of constructive dynamic work are to be seen not so much from a technological and rational point of view than as free play with mechanical elements. As in the creation of mobiles, the problem here is one of transforming technical elements into art.

We begin with the simplest motion play. Vibration, swing in opposite directions, is a natural process (quaking-grass) to be discovered and taken as a model for these exercises. The material is drawn wire, which is harder and more elastic than soft wire.

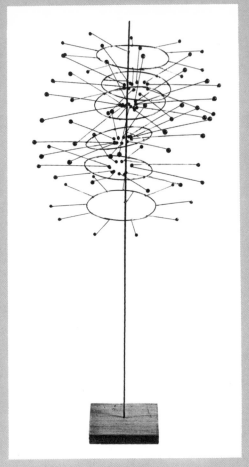

366 S

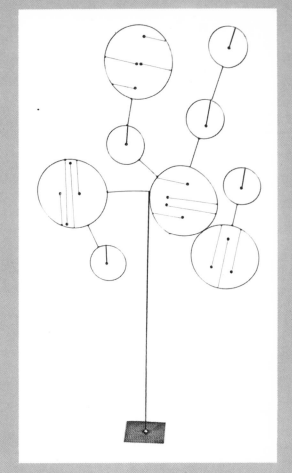

367 S

363-365: Various forms of motion play. A slight push will set these figures vibrating, the movement being more pronounced in those with wooden spheres at the ends. Width and duration of the vibration depend on the material, the length of the arms and on the weights.

366: Steel balls of different sizes cause stronger vibration. Brass wire, drawn.

367: Mobile consisting of several circular shapes which move at the slightest touch. Height, 24″; drawn brass wire.

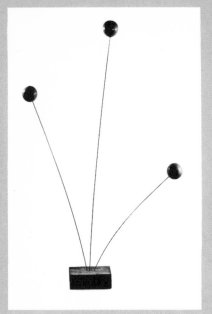

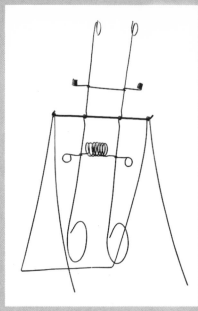

368

369 S

370 S

The pendulum offers further possibilities for dynamic constructions.

368: Wooden balls fastened to the ends of hard spring wire. The longer the arm, the wider and longer the swing.

369, 370: Two solutions to the problem, 'pendulum'. Material: galvanized steel wire.

371: A wire frame holds a wavy crankshaft to which six connecting-rods crowned with glass balls have been fastened. As the crank turns, the balls swing in different rhythms.

372: The grotesque, insect-like movements of this 'machine' show technical imagination as well as a good sense of form.

373: 'Foundry', created by a boy of 15.

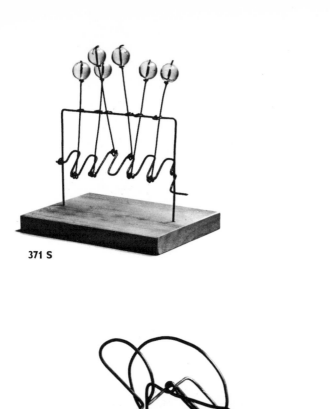

371 S

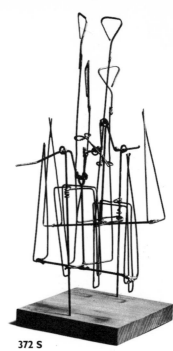

372 S

373 B 15

113

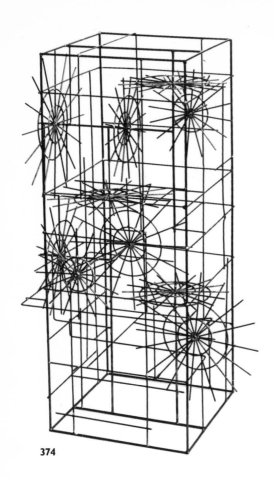

374

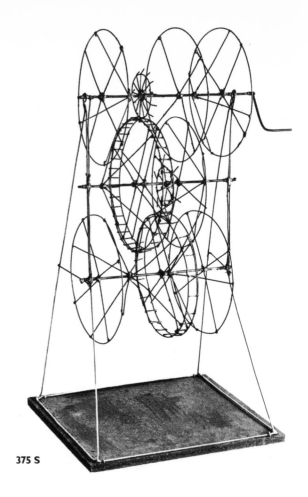

375 S

374: An oblong frame contains, on different levels, shafts firmly connected to cog-wheels. Small brass pipes serve as bearings for the shafts. The work convinces by its unity of form, function and construction. The connections are soldered.

375: Movement and counter-movement of gears on three levels.

376: Differentiated movements within a spherical object.

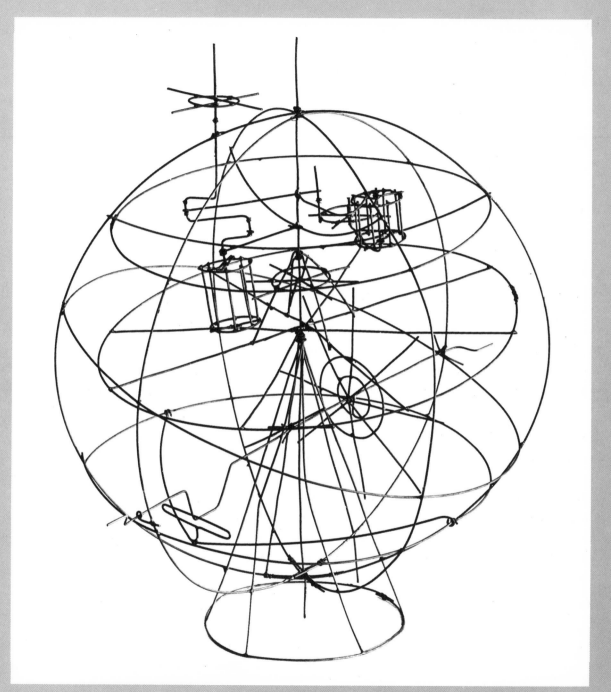

376 S

TECHNICAL TIPS

MATERIALS

According to their qualities, metals fall into the following groups: iron and steel, non-ferrous metals, light metals and precious metals. Among the non-ferrous metals are copper, brass, zinc, lead and bronze. Aluminium is the commonest of light metals. Gold, silver and platinum are among the precious metals. Metals are available as semi-manufactured products. For the purposes of this book, wire, wire fabric and tin are the most suitable materials.

WIRE

Wires may be soft, medium and hard. They are made of a variety of metals and in many different sizes. The commonest is galvanized steel (iron) wire, obtainable in the shape of rings and rods and especially suitable for bending and soldering, as it is flexible and not subject to rust. Annealed steel wire (binding wire) is softer and will rust in time. Its blue colour is due to oxide.

Aluminium wire is very soft and bends easily. Hammering on a metal block shows it to be tough and malleable. Suitable thicknesses: 1-2.5 mm.

Copper, brass and copper-plated wires are suitable for wire jewellery. We use mainly soft and medium-hard wires in thicknesses of 0.8-1.5 mm. Copper is an element, brass an alloy of copper and zinc.

Steel spring wire is very hard and does not bend easily. Welded steel wire is copper-plated as a protection against rust. It is obtainable in the shape of rods and in various thicknesses.

TIN

For simple tin work, sheet iron, galvanized sheet iron, zinc plate, tin plate and aluminium plate are the most suitable materials. They should be as soft as possible and not too thick, so as to be easily workable. Tin plate is galvanized sheet iron. It is rust-free and easily soldered and may be obtained in thicknesses of 0.15-1 mm. Tin which is less than 0.2 mm thick is called foil. Aluminium foil is very suitable for embossing. Chased vessels are best made of soft copper plate, 0.8-1 mm thick. Brass and pinckbeck are also suitable. Lead can be easily bent and hammered but should be handled with caution. Traces of lead may adhere to the fingers and cause damage to health. After working with lead, it is absolutely necessary to wash one's hands before eating.

FABRIC

Wire fabric may be of steel, brass or copper. Galvanized sheet iron fabric is most common for use in metal work. The fabric is woven of fine wires. The weave depends on the width of the mesh and the thickness of the wire. Wire fabric with a mesh of 0.8 mm and a thickness of 0.25 mm is classed among the fine fabrics. A soldered fabric, as used, for instance, in the building trade, is suitable as a background to figurative wire work (see illustrations 97-99).

116

METHODS

BENDING OF WIRE AND TIN

Soft wire and tin may be bent by hand. Angling is done by flat-nosed pliers, rounding by round-nosed pliers. Round stakes are also used to achieve uniformity. Wavy strips of tin are shaped by means of a bending frame, i.e. round wooden stakes pegged down on a board. The angling is done with a mallet or plastic hammer. The tin is held in a clamp or placed on a bending bar or iron girder. A special kind of bench is required for bending longer pieces of tin. For cylindrical shapes, the tin is bent round a strong stake or pipe section held in a vice.

THE COURSING OF VESSELS

This process requires an engineer's hammer and a block of beech wood with a round groove. Beginning with the bottom edge, the tin is folded on the block and subsequently hammered out again at right angles to the folds. Folding, straightening, stretching and compressing continues until the desired shape has been achieved. After each process the tin must be annealed and pickled.

EMBOSSING AND CHASING

Aluminium foil is the most suitable material for embossing. Round, pointed sticks of hardwood, ballpoint pens or pencils may be used to press out lines and surfaces on a soft pad of folded newspaper. Thin tin of up to 0.3 mm thick lends itself to chasing. The punches can be home-made of welded wire or nails by filing their points square, round or ball-shaped. Strong cardboard or hardboard may be used as a pad.

PUNCHING

Thin aluminium or welded tin are suitable for punching with nails or other pointed objects on a soft board. Thicker tin requires a hardwood pad.

DRILLING

The piece to be drilled must be firmly fixed in a clamp, so that it cannot turn with the drill. The centre of the borehole is marked and countersunk to prevent the drill from straying. Hand or electric drills may be used.

SAWING

A metal saw bites on the forward stroke. The blades are interchangeable. The piece to be sawn is placed in the clamp in such a way that the cut is close to the jaws and at the back end of the metal. A fret saw with a metal blade is recommended for finer work.

FILING

Files vary in length, type of cut, shape and cross section. In general, we use a coarse file first and then a smooth-cut. The piece to be worked must be firmly held by the clamp to prevent it springing back.

SOLDERING AND BRAZING

For cold-soldering we need the following tools and materials: an electric soldering-iron (80 and 150 watt), solder, flux and sal-ammoniac. A durable bit is better value than the simple copper bit. It does not smoulder, keeps its shape, is easily exchanged and needs no 'tinning', i.e. cleaning with sal-ammoniac or a file. The pieces to be soldered are cleaned of oxide, grease and dirt with a file and emery-cloth, and flux is applied. The soldered pieces must not be moved until the solder has set hard. The following metals may be cold-soldered: welded tin, galvanized tin, galvanized sheet iron, copper and brass. Aluminium cannot be soldered.

Hard-soldering or brazing with a blow-pipe requires higher temperatures and is more durable than cold-soldering.

Various tools, such as blow-pipe, soldering gun or a welding-torch set to a gentle heat, may be used. The solder or spelter is an alloy of copper and silver, and borax is used as flux. The melting point of modern hard spelters lies around 700° C. (1292° F.). No flux is required for soldering copper.

RIVETING

Metal pieces, such as tin, etc., are firmly joined by rivets of soft metal (aluminium, copper) which is easily flattened with a hammer. Rivets are available in various sizes with round or flat heads. The work requires a hammer, rivet set and metal support. The rivet consists of head and shaft. The processes involved in riveting are drilling or punching, preforming and beating out of the rivet head. When the rivet is inserted into the drilled hole, the shaft should protrude a little.

STRAIGHTENING WIRE AND TIN

Wire that has been wound round a reel becomes rigid when straightened out. Fix one end firmly in a clamp, grip the other end with a pair of flat-nosed pliers and give several strong jerks. Bent tin is straightened by means of a mallet, rubber or plastic hammer on a support of flat steel or an anvil.

SOFTENING METAL

Hammering, bending and stretching affect the structure of metal and make it harder and more brittle. It must be heated to restore its original structure. This may be done with a Bunsen burner or blow-pipe, and the resulting particles of burnt metal should be removed with a pickle consisting of one part sulphuric acid to ten parts of water. Copper, brass and mild steel may be cooled in water.

GRINDING AND POLISHING

Grinding is done with an emery-cloth. For very fine work, put a drop of oil on the cloth. Steel wool and some pastes are also suitable. Polishing agents should be applied with a soft cloth.

SURFACE TREATMENT AND PROTECTION

A special lacquer protects metal from stains and corrosion. The metal is cleaned of grease and oil and the lacquer applied with a soft brush. Copper, brass and pinchbeck may be tinted with a solution of sulphate of potash. The metal is submerged in the solution until the desired colour appears.

Note on materials: There are several different standards to which sheet metal and wire are made. The Brown & Sharpe Gauge is common in the United States; according to its scale, 1 gauge (ga.) is equivalent to 7.341 mm or 0.289 in, and the higher the gauge, the smaller the measurement.